World Stage Press
Verse from the Village

Southern Spiced: A Brown Girl's Tale

Poems by
Felicia Taylor E.

World Stage Press
Verse from the Village

World Stage Press
Verse from the Village

Southern Spiced: A Brown Girls Tale
© 2021, Felicia Taylor E.
ISBN: 978-1-952952-19-7

First Edition, 2021

Printed in the United States of America

Cover Design by "Jade" Fuqi Sun
Layout Design by Krystle May Statler

Dedicated to Nse and Nicholas

Della Mae, Ruth, James, Jason and Daisy

My Angels: Jamie, "Daddy" Buster, Mother Jessie,

Daddy Revous and Uncle Don

&

My Family

Contents

Piney Woods Time

Blues of Life and Love

Grateful

Intro

Southern Spiced Brown Girl

I'm excited to peel back layers of my life and share my heart, my fears and woes. Most of which only Daisy, my dear diary has had the pleasure of hearing. As you turn the next pages, I hope you feel the warm welcome as you journey through the doors of my life.

Beginning

Afterschool Sitters

My babysitter's Ernie and Bert brought me
laughter and Count Dracula inspired me to write numbers in
my notebook. The Sesame neighborhood gave me warmth and
protection. I learned words, numbers and the good
neighborhood ways of life on *Sesame Street*.

I moved my head to the fun activities of the Electric Company
while problem solving. Saying the word-problem out
loud was my fun learning time!

R-ug! Rug!

B-at! Bat!

Super Heroes solved word-problems while everything
moved with a swirl of excitement.

Zoom zoom, zooma zoom was the time for the last sitter that
watched me before my Mom came home
from work.

Learning recipes and all about science
was my favorite time!

At the end of their show, I rushed to write their address on paper
when they shared it by song. I'd hope each time, I'd get it
right and figure out how to send them a letter.

"Write *Zoom*. Z-double-O-M. Box 3-5-0. Boston,
Mass 0-2-1-3-4: Send it to ZOOM!"

After the school bus dropped me off, I had my pen and paper in hand, and eagerly took my sitters' instructions until Mom came home from work.

Dedicated to
PBS Programming

Stand In the Corner

My family sent me to school at the early age of four
being bored of learning all I could from tv, I begged to go.

I was smart
sat upright in my chair always raised my hand to give an
answer or ask a question. Finished my work as soon as the
teacher handed it out and helped her
in the classroom too.

It was the 1st Grade where I first played kickball, had tetherball
battles and placed my hand over my heart for the Pledge of
Allegiance.

I wore ruffled pinafore dresses, white lace trimmed socks
with black patent leather shoes. Dressed differently from the
other girls. They could wear shorts with cute shirts, colorful
tops with matching pants.

One day my class went to Storytime in the Teacher's class next
door. All the students sat with legs criss-crossed on the floor,
waiting to hear the new adventure. As soon as the story
began, two students began talking.

When the Teacher stopped the story and asked, "Who was
talking?"
No one answered. I raised my hand, and pointed
to who was talking.

"Slap!"

The green-eyed Teacher used her open hand and knocked
the entire right side of my face. It felt like hot needles on my
face and sent rattles of waves in my head.

An uncomfortable silence choked the room.
"*No one asked you!*" she said with a dripping angry voice. Her stern words further burned the stinging on my face. "*Go to the corner, and put your nose to the wall!*" I stood at the wall with my back to the class.

I could feel their stares on my back. The tears that swelled and tried to come out, were pulled back deep inside.
From that corner spot, I listened to the rest of the story, and wondered why my answer was at fault?

I was confused; what had I done wrong? What made the mean, green-eyed Teacher be so angry to caused her to hurt and embarrass me in front of the class? I understood later she had no affection for a child like me.

Although integration had been mandated by the Brown vs Board act in 1954, which cited that racial segregation of children in public schools unconstitutional, our town still practiced segregation up until the 1960's.

A few years before this change in our schools, our President John F. Kennedy and Civil Rights Leader, Dr. Martin Luther King Jr. had been killed because of their resilient power, fight for rights and their opinions of equality and their opinions of inequality for many.

And for many, like this mean hearted Teacher, the acceptance of equality for all was too difficult to accept and approve.

But, she didn't silence my voice.

Dedicated to
Bobo for remembering
Denton Segregation article cited from, desegratingdenton.omeka.net
Brown vs. Board of Education article cited history.com

I Am Pippi

I had a strict routine after school:
leap carefully from the bus exit steps, run into the store, grab
snacks and let the store cashier list my items on the tally of
the "owe me list." Chips, a drink and a Seven Up candy bar,
which was like a box of chocolates in one bar to me.

This was put on a tab, and when Mom came home, she'd
stop to settle the bill. But, before either
my parents arrived,

I was PIPPI!

Throwing pots under cabinets so I didn't have to scrub
them clean. And climbing through barbed wire fences
to grab wild flowers in the empty pasture while
chasing butterflies.

My adorable monkey, Mr. Nilson always leaped from
cabinet to cabinet around the kitchen
in my imagination.

I even imagined Pippi's horse running around in the
pasture next to the house. And if I needed him to gallop
to me, I only had to whis-tle LOUD.

My Dad wasn't a pirate off on the seven seas, but he
was away at work, like Pippi's Dad. And even though

Mom was coming home only a few hours after school, she
was still in another place, like Pippi's mom.

And with my imaginary friends, I was never alone.
One special day, I became a cake creator

and made a chocolate cake from my own recipe!
Quite a feat at 7 years old, I'd say!

I am Pippi Longstockings!
If you say it fast it's Sil-ly!
Hair in pigtails and a big smile on my face,
climbing up trees and running free.
I am PIPPI all the way!

Mi-ss-i-ss-i-pp-i

In the back of the Monte Carlo,
I sat with a rod across the backseat full of
clothes for our move to Mississippi from Texas.
Hooked to the bumper was a small U-Haul container.

Sitting on luggage and boxes,
I pretended the clothing around me
was a tent. I slept, rode passenger-style
and hopped out at places to
stretch with Mom and Dad.

In the new state of Mississippi,
I learned about the musical group
Sonny and Cher. Spanish rolled
from my tongue easier, and we
moved into our first apartment.

The mock Sonny and Cher we met were
a couple that always seemed totally in love.
My parents said they were hippies,
beings of love and peace.
A nice couple that reminded them
of the singing duo, "Sonny & Cher."

Sonny had mushroom shaped brown hair,
circular deep brown eyes and a bushy mustache.
Cher wore lovely sleek dresses,
had long dark hair past her shoulders,
deep dark eyes and a beaming smile.

She often laid out to tan in the sun
with a two-piece bathing suit.
Evenings we spent outside with them,
me in the pool and my Parents
talking or toasting their glasses with Sonny and Cher.

A year later we moved to Brownsville, Texas.
Some Saturday's my Parents and I drove
across the border and went to Mexico.

We sat inside dark restaurants and clubs.
Ate tacos and cheese covered enchiladas with
sides of beans and rice.

I drank Shirley Temples, a mix of
Coca-Cola and cherries and my
parents had adult drinks.

We'd shop at the mini stores buying colorful
woven blankets, ornately embroidered
shirts and magic Mexican jumping beans.
As nighttime fell upon us, we'd hop back into
the car and across the border to go
back home.

Jumping beans in my hand, I felt the magic
vibrations, as the beans radiated in my grasp as
we crossed out of Mexico and back home.

Dedicated to
Mom & Dad and our adventures

Creek Bed

When the Creek bed is full and flowing to
the brim, it becomes rushing waves of water and
creates a slippery slope.

Though it is not the best time to search
for crawdads or search
for shiny rocks,

I delight in the fast movement and the
crashing sounds of the water
licking upon each current.

There can be danger in this water flow, but
listening to it brings a peaceful and
hypnotic sound. Rain causes the creek
waters to rush and rise above
the thick muddy banks.

It displaces, cleanses and regenerates. The
greenness gets brighter and debris is
cleaned away. Rainfall stops and
all settles when the water level goes
down as the water
flows slowly again.

That's when I swish down the red dirt slide and
dunk my feet around. I glide upon the rocks. Eye to foot
coordination becomes a natural feat. No slip
and fall on my watch! As I survey the floor
bed, I spy something moving. Standing as still as
a one legged ostrich, I search for my
creek gems to capture and collect.

My legs stand stark still and I toss my head to
knock my bangs out of my sight. A flurry
of dark brown dirt swirls and shows my
eyes where to follow.

Out popped a small reddish brown crawdad
digging down into the floor, trying to
go deeper inside. My knees bend
down real swift and I grabbed
it up right quick!

Carefully holding the middle with three fingers,
I avoid the pinchers so they
don't snap my finger.

And inside it went! Straight into my silver minnow
bucket with just a bit of creek water.
A trick I learned from my Dad.

Sloshing through the creek in my white cotton
tennis shoes. My toes swished left to
right, feeling grit and grainy
of dirt inside.

The sun beams in the west, while
shadows sing from the hills.

♪ ♪ ♪

Crawfish are a plenty!
You can find them day or night. Get the eye
of a seeker and their pincher won't bite.
Keep looking for the gold, beyond the
rainbow. In the creek you'll find it,
where the rocks do glow.

♪ ♪ ♪

Right next to the shimmery auburn rock, I see a
teeny tiny fish! A tiny dark grey and black catfish
scrubbing the bottom floor with its whiskers,
flicks a fin and darts left. I smile and keep
on walking as the water flops by.

I pick up the blazing orange stone to add
to my rock gem collection.

And the Crawdad and I have a little talk.
Then I let it go free.

Twirly Whirly Tornado

When that twirly whirly comes to my town, we all
know what to do.

We get under a doorway and place our writing hand into
the crook of our opposite arm to protect that hand.

If you're a rightie? The right hand goes right to left. A
leftie does the opposite.

Next, our left or right palm over the base of our neck, and
head bent down. Teachers say that our spine and neck
get protected this way if we're struck by
something from above.

When at school and the whirly wind comes through
our heavens and from the sky, we rush to the hallway,
place our back to the wall, sit side by side, crisscross on
the floor and take the position like I said before.

At home we do things differently.

On the news we live in a danger zone. A trailer park is
kinda the toppling place for tornado whirls.
Knocking and throwing everything around.

Tree trunks uproot from the ground, and trailer home
tops are often pulled right off.

My Mom sends me to hide in the bathtub and she stands
under the bathroom door frame. They are both the safest
places to be if the structure is pulled away.

Most times when we hear it's coming, we hop in the car and go to Mother Jessie's, my Grandmom. Her place is safer, because it's higher ground.

Sometimes you can just feel that the whirly-whirl is gonna come!

Everything feels quiet and still. A dark grey and black fog covers the sky. And trembling sounds are heard from the shivering leaves of the trees.

Once, I layed on the ground and reached my hand up to the sky. I hoped to be swept up by the Texas tornado. Escaping and twirling 'round above the clouds like Dorothy in the *Wizard of Oz*.

I knew in my spirit that Brown girls could fly too, and land in a magical place, just like Oz.

Gone with the Wind

Movietime is popcorn, kernels poppin' in hot oil over a
flame lit stove, jumping and exploding inside an overused
silver metal pot in our kitchen.

Melted butter poured on top and shaker
salt spices it up!

We dress in comfy clothes, and most times I have my
warm cotton pajamas on.

Hopping in the black and grey Monte Carlo with the wheels
spinning on the ground, Dad's car has style. We hit the
graveled road and ventured up the curve
on Ft. Worth Drive.

Not far from our trailer park lot where we live alone is the
Drive-in movie theater. This night as we drive up, the
marquee lit up like New York City lights:

GONE WITH THE WIND
starring
Vivien Leigh and Clark Gable

Sometimes my Parents pay the entry for all three
of us. And sometimes they pay the entry
fee just for them.

It was those times I'd hide below a blanket with a freshly
popped popcorn pot. My 7yr-old or 8yr-old self lying down
on the floorboard in the darkness in the backseat of the car.
And I envision being a spy or in a movie of my own.

Past the ticket check in, we drove to find a parking spot. Cars
parked side by side and lined up row by row. We find an
empty sound speaker, park beside it and
attach it to our window.

Sometimes I get quite bored or just can't see the screen
from the backseat that well. My parents would let me lie
on the hood so I could have a closer view.

Play areas for kids are to the corner of the movie screen.
The concession stand is always filled with people.
They stand in lines to buy hotdogs, popcorn,
cheese nachos, soda pop or Cracker Jacks.

I watch the screen and love the velvet and blouson
dress that Scarlet O'Hara wore.

Everyone gasps as she ripped a velvety deep emerald green
panel from the curtains and had it sewn into
a fashionable and gorgeous velvet gown.

She figured out how to turn lemons into lemonade. And how
to survive when her money "was funny"
as my Aunt would say.

Her admirer Rhett Butler loved her, but Scarlett
loved another man. In the end
that was her end.
We turn the volume up on the speaker as loud
as we can when Rhett and Scarlet are
having an argument.

Our view is blocked by a few concession stand patrons
that walk in front of our car to return to their cars. As
soon as they close their car door, we hear Rhett
Butler say to Scarlett as he walked out the door,

"Frankly my dear, I dont give a damn!"

This is the 1st time I've heard a curse word in
a movie! And a phrase I'd never forget.

Bad words were not allowed to be spoken
by kids in my family, but whenever we
passed by the marquee and I saw the
name of the movie still there,
my head would say what
my mouth never could:

"Frankly, My Dear, I-dont-give-a-Damn!"

Dedicated to
the Drive-in Movies
Ft. Worth Drive, Denton, Texas

Fire In My Head

Up the mulberry tree, laying on a branch
berries eaten, yummy-yum,
gobbled up so fast.

Found a squiggly worm, lost my appetite.
Spit the berries out of my mouth.
Then slid down the rugged trunk,
and laid with my back upon the ground.

Fire ants crawled through my scalp, and chomped me up.
Pulling at my hair, I ran screaming to the house.
Mom washed my burning head and put the biting fire out!

Ode to Billy The Kid

An outlaw lived beyond our hills in Denton, Texas.

Billy the Kid was his name.
Young and brash, pistol toting
and slingin' cowboy.

He'd been added to the Wanted posters.

Running in packs of outlaws or alone, he was known for
robbing. Mostly stage coaches and banks and such.

After the job was done they'd run to the hills to hide from the
Marshall and the Law:

Our home sat on the cusp of these hills. Beyond the creek
beds, flat lands and the railroad tracks.

Some days I really felt like Billy. Especially when my mom
made me wear dresses to my knees.

Ruffled underwear underneath it, lace white socks and black
patent leather shoes.

My hair is separated into ponytails, "pigtails" we call them.
And white ribbons tied perfectly on each.

At school, I played and ran around with all my might and
waited in line for the tether ball matches.

But my dress and shoes slowed me down a bit.
Got snagged on trees, and scuffed during kickball time.

This school day would become a special day that would go down in the family book.

I stepped down from the bus and walked to my front door.

Mom screamed "What happened?" My prim and proper look was no longer there.

My dress ruffle had parted from the seams. A ponytail was braided, one unbraided. Even one of my white ribbons is gone.

My bangs no longer curled, were flat on my face and wet with sweat. Along with my patent leather shoes scuffed on both sides.

"I wanted to play. And I can't in this dress."

Dad looked up and said, "I'm sick of this mess! Let's go get some jeans!"

"Jeans?" screamed Mom. Then poor Mom burst into tears. Dad and I hopped in the Monte Carlo and drove to the Army & Navy surplus store.

And guess what? I got a pink jean jacket with matching jeans and a light periwinkle blue jacket with jeans to match too.

On the clothing label inside it said "Billy the Kid."

Dedicated to
my Dad and his love of Westerns

A Few of my Favorite Things

Playing Monopoly at the dining table with my family.

Learning and understanding poker moves to play with Dad to practice his poker hand.

Eating breakfast for dinner, my favorite!

Having silver dollar pancakes at IHOP Pancake House while Mom had her famous club sandwich because she wasn't a breakfast person, and Dad ate his 3-stack of pancakes.

Drinking my smoke signaled hot cocoa topped with whipped cream.

Having Mom's strawberry shortcake for dessert. Going to Baskin & Robbins and getting pralines & cream or french vanilla with Dad and strawberry shortcake ice cream with Mom.

Fishing times at the wharf with a new fishing pole.

Six Flags yearly trips every year and riding every ride from opening to close.

And traveling on the road, visiting family and friends in Fort Worth, Lewisville or the Dallas area.

Running wild with laughter and having awesome play time with them.

Eating raw oysters for the first time.

Going to the *Southern Kitchen* for their seven course dinner and other restaurants to test their menu.

Enjoying Shirley Temples when Mom and Dad had the adult drink.

Being allowed to make decisions on my own later in life.

Learning how to change my oil, tires and put antifreeze in my car.

Mom and Dad are always figuring a way out of No way.

A Biblical Name

My Mom has a biblical name. There's a book of Ruth in the Bible and she has similar ways. Kind, faithful and loving. Always giving and sharing what she has.

She has always found favor like the biblical Ruth for her gifts of choice and behavior.

She's also a bundle of shininess. Glowing spirit and laughter surrounds her.

Shiny shoes with crystals like rainbows fill her closet space, my favorite place to play.

She loves Doris Day attire, and I *Love Lucy* is her twin.

Her creative flair is in her clothes, her home and all throughout her core.

Her giddiness and positivity gives a "you can do it" attitude!

Loving with care and giving.

Goodness all wrapped up into one.

That's my *Mom*

You Savvy?

Watching Westerns on Saturday is a chosen art. John Wayne, Clint Eastwood and the Rifleman is how it starts.

Different kinds of music is what he likes. Bobby Blue Bland, Kool & The Gang, Marvin Gaye, and Teddy Pendergrass.

His favorites were the top ones on the radio. Every payday, albums were bought and spinned upon the large pecan wooden stereo.

The best collection and the best record player around.

Poker is his game of choice. Dominoes doesn't fall far behind, and other cards, but he also played Monopoly with me.

And taught me how to find a worm in the ground to hook on the fishing pole. Patiently sitting for the croppy, carp, perch or catfish to bite.

Buffalo had too much bone, I didn't eat that one.

Once there were frog legs brought from the lake.

We fried them up and tried them for the first time.

We never repeated it again, it was their frog legs sticking from the plate.

He sometimes bellows like a bear and has his roaring time. But he'll give you the shirt off his back,
taking care of all those that he loves.

Santa Fe *for life* driving as an Engineer.

He's finally flowing through life with his family in his style.

No longer asking if you're savvy anymore
because he knows he's savvy for us all.

That's my *Dad*

Touch of My Hair

You reaching a nervous hand forward,
as if I was an animal to pet at a zoo
You touched my hair to feel something
different to you
Hands and eyes surrounded me, like a
tiger waiting to consume
its vulnerable prey
Standing still
Breathing heavy

I wished you had asked me
how I felt before you reached
out, or before you said
what you said.
"She's Black!"
Those words bounced in my head
like a kangaroo at the boxing match.

"We've only seen them on tv!"

My brown eyes and mind,
soaked in your words,
as my spirit started to sink

My Girl Scout troop didn't know
what to think. I was the
only black Girl Scout on
our camping trip.

But, when the circling around me became
intense, and the touching was
invasive and uncomfortable.

Our Troop leader asked us to
step out from the group. Say goodbye
and move on out. I don't know why I didn't
receive a Patch for my bravery that day,
because I deserved it.

Dedicated to
those that are different

Mirror Test

Mom is my hairstylist; she's brushed
and coiffed my hair in many ways.

Press and curl and ponytails. Bun on top
with curly kisses on my sides and perfect bangs
and puffy loops.

She clips my hair on the fullness of the moon,
'cause my Grandmother said that helps the hair grow
long and strong.

It's only on special times I get to
wear my hair down, and sweep it
back with a ribbon to add a pretty effect.

My Grandmom also styles it just right, even
if the bands on my ponytails feel kinda tight. And
my Aunt Dede braids it really cool, with flair designs
and my initials, monogrammed in the back.

But there are two people that I love very much that
can't style my hair the way I want.

Uncle Laurance sometimes helps if Mom is late for work.
He makes homemade biscuits kinda good, but his hair
combing skills aren't done my way. It's technically
ponytails he creates, but they look uneven and
point to the sky.

My Aunt Faye doesn't try to pass the test.
I ask for bangs and she won't create them
even when I ask. I guess she doesn't understand
how, because she has no girls, just my cousins Mark and Chad.

Of all that have styled my hair,
Mom is the best and always
passes my mirror test.

The Mouse and the Cheese

Mentioning the name Mouse makes
my Mom's heart scream!

Today my parents went to the store,
and my cousin Stephanie and I were left behind.

"I can catch a mouse," I told her.
"A mouse?"
"Yes, a mouse. It lives under the fridge!"
"Under your fridge?" she said, pointing at it.
"Yes. It'll come out as soon as I bring out some cheese."
"Ok. How we gonna trap it?"

I hadn't really planned this out.
But, I always had very brilliant ideas.
Like when I made a Rabbit trap
to catch a brown and white Cottontail.

It began with a cardboard box. And then a
small branch off the sycamore tree. I tilted the box up,
with the stick propping up the front.
Tossed in a few carrots in the back.
Next day, no Bunny.
Carrots gone and box still up.
Hadn't thought that one out very well.

"This time, I got it!!" I said.
"You do?" she smiled.
I hopped to grab the clear glass blender top.
It served as a tunnel shape and the mouse could be caught!
I got the cheese, put it in. Dimmed the light.
Mouse came out!

Wait?

How would it stay inside? I ran to
grab a drinking cup and pop! It became a top.

We waited.
And waited.
Just laid on the floor, not breathing, not blinking.
And then the cute mouse ran Out!

It sniffed the cheese without a nibble,
then scattered back to hide again!

I Wish

Too bad he didn't know me.
I think he would have liked me well.
But then again maybe he couldn't;
he didn't know himself.

Too bad he didn't know me,
I think I could have made him smile.
I did for my friends and
the strangers that I came upon.

I wish that he had known me.
From inside out and all my good inside.

But he often overflowed with frustrations.

When that's not balanced, it causes stress
and high powered yells.

But once, he did know me
when my needs were just milk
and a diaper change.
And he'd borrow a dollar to feed me,
and for him that
seemed a bit hard to admit

I wish that he had known me,
He could have gleaned how bright I beamed

Independence is Like A Flower

A Sunflower blooms alone.
It's forced to be capable
and sturdy on its own.

A Rose can look independently beautiful alone,
but needs bushels of petals around for an orchestra tune,
flourishing and dependent on those around
it to lend support.

I am a Sunflower, forced to be capable, sturdy, tall and
independently on my own.

Their Best

They loved me the best way they knew how.
Provided me with all they felt they could.

We traveled together and shared the same cup.
That impressed many families that we
stopped to by to visit,
"You don't want another glass?" they'd often ask.
"No, we'll drink out of this one," my Dad would respond.

We were a posse that took care of each other.
Also functioning by ourselves very well.

"You're an independent child," they've always said.

Paper Chase

Who-Hoo!
We went on a chase today.
Like riding in a getaway car down the freeway to anywhere I
want to go!
"You took a number," my Mom said.
"I didn't." my Dad said.
"I saw it!"
"No, you did not."
"Let me see your pants pocket!"

Dad reached in and pulled something out.
My eyes and head went back & forth, then to & fro.
"I saw the paper, it's got a number.

Give that to me!"
"No. It's not a number or a piece of paper"

Out the door he vanished and hopped
into his Roadrunner GTO.
We took off close behind him in Mom's silver Thunderbird.

His wheels peeled out like *Smokey & The Bandit*.
We whirled out, wheels screeching, right behind him!

He took the back roads from our house and Mom followed.
She was on his trail like white on rice, like a cat nabbing a bird
or fish gobbling a tadpole!

He sped up and she sped up some more.
With his headlights bouncing off the darkness, our lights
bounced from the rear of his car.

We thought his hand flew out of the driver's side of the GTO.
"Was that his hand out the window?"
"He threw something out Mom. I think it's thrown out!"

The adventurer in me pined to stop and search for that
"supposed item" we thought we had seen,
both cars kept moving, like race cars pushing for the finish line.
Lights bounced off the dark trees and the road we traveled,
and Dad spun his car towards home.

A crescent moon watched as our pace began slowing,
and the chase now led us home.

Uncle Tom, Uncle Tom!

Uncle Tom!
You are an Uncle, Uncle Tom!

Little Brown girl, do you know you're Brown?
You should know your place and know who
at school to hang around.

Stop flouncing everywhere, thinking
you can be with everyone.
You're no better, we're brown just like you.

We think you forgot your place, brown girl!

Let us explain for you:
Light brown, brown or ebony brown
Any shade or any hue, we are all pretty too!

Stop walking around with those white skin folks,
thinking you can do what they do.

You think that you're better than what you are
or more better than us?

Then you are an Uncle Tom through and through!
Cause that's how Uncle Tom's think
and how they do.

Stop spending' time with them at recess and
lunch, 'cause we say so.

Or we'll throw you in that cabin, you Uncle Tom.
And keep you locked there too!

Echoes In My Spirit

They stood with white long robes on and a pointed white cap
like a dunce hat, but made of cloth.

Eyes peering out from the holes they had cut through
the front of the cloth.

Messages on the signs were a blur. As if flashes of lightning
blinded my view. I saw segments of words.

NO
NAACP
BLACKS
GO
HOME
KKK

My body was screaming from the seatbelt. Lock the door!
Run the light! Get away, Mama. Get away!
I couldn't believe that the people who call themselves the Klu
Klux Klan were standing on the corner in my town.
Upset that there was a NAACP Convention being
hosted at the Denton Convention Center.
No one was stopping them. And no one was there
to help me or my Mom.

A four way stop.
The station wagon had come to a halt
right next to where they grimaced and growled.
"Mom! Lock the doors."
"For what?"
"They're there!"

I screamed at the passenger window,
fearing the white gowned and hooded ones.
I'd read about their hatefulness in books. Seen their
destructiveness in movies. Felt they would harm
us when they saw our brown skin.

Their presence was always representative
of rampant evil, viciously
blaring hatred and death.

Cowardly covering their identity whilst always
having multiple attackers against just one.

My Mother's actions and not her reply is what
echoes in my spirit now.
"Ignore them. Don't be afraid."

She stared straight ahead. Didn't rush
to lock the doors.
We sat at the red light.

They stood on the corner next to us. Holding
their signs higher in the air.
Eyes behind hoods staring out.

I had not known that day that my Mom
had experienced these times
before. She had seen these white hood
covered ones in the past. They
weren't a shock to her. She had experienced
this and witnessed more than I ever would.

Marching for Civil Rights in the 60's with
Martin Luther King Jr., and
a member of the NAACP since youth.

This day of white covered sheets on head and
body would not deter her or us from
getting to our destination.

Today was not a day for them to win.
It was a time for the ones that *hid*
behind the white gowns and
hats to stand with their signs.
And be the ones in *hiding*.

As we drove past them in our car
and went on with our night,
I saw my mother match eyes
with the last of the hoods,

then she placed her focus on the road ahead.

Dedicated to
Mom and the strength of women

Piney Woods Time

Heavenly Peacock

Strutting my stuff is what I do
You see my plume expands beyond the rays of sunshine
A brilliance of cobalt blues, turquoise green
and golden yellows, circle
the eyes upon the feathers
that you behold.

I glide with pleasure, from the gaping eyes
that consume my majesty,

A pheasant like no other
seemingly to me, not in a birdly category at all

When you see me, you're peering at a glow of heaven
With a flash of fluffed out feathers,
spreading like an angel's wings

Dedicated to
the Lufkin Zoo where I first saw a lovely Peacock
Lufkin, Texas

Culverhouse

On weekend mornings we heard strong horses galloping
down the street, clomp-clomping on
the black gravel-paved road.

As riders pass by my Grandmom's house, I wish I were atop to
glide up on the horse's back and feel the wind upon my face,
as it begins a new glump-glump sound as now two riders are
in the saddle.

Excitement was always around when I came for long visits at
my grandparents' home, my second home. Kids walked or
rode their bikes up and down the streets.

We didn't travel too much, not even to the grocery store. But
we always had fun at home. And if we didn't get the cookies
that had been advertised on tv, we didn't' shrug shoulders or
huff under our breath. We were happy with what we had.

We'd eat and dance with sugar saturating our body and
smiles on our faces, because we had goodies at home.
We could have a few sweets a day, and only one at
dinner, either soda pop or some choice of cake or pie.

No two sugars could be eaten together.
Too many sweets and the worms would get 'cha.

"You gonna get the worms!" my Grandmom would say. And
then the magic mixture of her ole-timey homegrown medical
recipes would be placed upon us.

Syrup and salt! "Yuck!" It was always yuck, but said to do
the trick. As it glided into our tummy, the worms came
for sugar and then Wham!

Salt mixed up with syrup killed them.
Sounds gross, but my Grandmom knows
a lot about the curing and what Mama says, goes!

Grandmom's Kitchen

As I lay in my Aunties full-size, oakwood four-poster bed,
beams of sun crash against my face, revealing
that nighttime is done.

Rolling on my side, still deep in sleepyville. My nose is tickled
with the scents of my Grandmom's kitchen. And a warmth of
familiarness fills me up.

Breakfast is the first meal, and an important one here. The
sound of hickory smoked bacon and flavorful, spiced sausage
sizzles and crackles in the pan.

Marinating and cooking within its own juices, to be later used
for gravy when the pork chops are cooked. Fresh eggs are
cracked clean and scrambled just right. I never know
how they orchestrate such a beautiful meal. But,
they are the Maestra's and we are the grateful
receivers of deliciousness.

Biscuits fill the house with fresh basked scents. Flour,
shortening and baking powder mix, rolled together and cut
into perfect circles with a glass cup. Rice is simmering and
cooked for 20 minutes.

Southern grits are on slow simmer as they bubble in the
smallest pot. And a side of butter is in the crystal butter
dish, waiting there, ready to top anything while it's
piping hot.

TJ Blackburn syrup, grape jelly or plum preserves are set on
the table. "Time for breakfast!" My Grandmom's say in either
house. Whether it's my Dad's Mom, "Mother Jessie" or my
Mom's Mom, "Mama."

All have awoken from their slumber. And loved ones gather around a freshly cooked meal as morning greetings are shared of "Good Morning" "Hope you slept well."

Grabbing plates, forks and spoons in preparation to pile servings of the delicious morning meal on our plates, we smile with love and gratitude as we eat to our belly's brim, often times too much.

Perfectly roasted coffee, hot Lipton Tea or fresh milk to wash it all down. The Mother Maestra's and Matriarch's have filled our bellies with food, and infused us all with love.

Dedicated to
my Grandmom's and their Southern cooking
Della Mae and Jessie Bell

Soul Train Sunday

We waited all week for Saturdays.
No *All My Children* or *Young and the Restless* on this day.
We slept a little late, ate our breakfast, watched children's
shows. Then at 11 o'clock? It was time for the *Sooooul Train!*

Rules were to clean before getting to play, so we swept
the floor as we watched and danced with broom
in hand, on our make believe *Soul Train* stage.

With dreamy eyes, we gazed and listened to the soulful
Disco and R&B Singers perform their new hits.

And we were mesmerized as the host Don Cornelius
interviewed each performer or group.

Chaka Khan gleamed her big warm smile and puffy-wide
reddish brown Afro styled hair; her persona
spoke musically before she hit a tune!

And the musical group *Switch*, new on the scene, glowed
with handsomeness. Their groovy style and hip clothes
were in sync with their harmonies. Smooth
voices sang "I call your name girl," just to me!

The train tooted it's horn off the program and
we were done with inside time.
After our room, the den and the bathroom were cleaned.
We dressed, washed our faces and brushed our hair neatly.
Sparkling fresh, we leaped out the door to go play in
the dusty dirt outside.

Through osmosis (or maybe it was calculated) after
Soul Train time, the other kids on the street always
came out to play at the same time as we did.
Dede and I went straight to our favorite play
area and they bustled over.

No boys were allowed. Only once, we let Junior play, who
came with his sisters, Sue Mara and Robbie. And
we'd help feed their Big Mama's cats
that lived next door to us.

Today, like on most days, we were building a house. One
bedsheet and a stick was what we had, and that was
lucky for my Grandmom to lend us a sheet.

Our playhouse was created in the vacant lot next to
our real home, with cloth tied and spread between
the thin small trees.

The sheet became a separator between the street and
our kid-built home. A stick or limb that we'd find on
the ground or break from a dead tree could mix
up some made-up dinner dishes. We often stirred
up a pretend meal in an old dented pot
or an old flower bed.

As the sun began to sink down in the sky, we knew it was
time to clean up and go inside for supper. We picked
up our things in our area, as we were all taught,
and said goodnight as we went inside to prepare for the
next day of Sunday school and church.

Dedicated to
Dede and the Neighborhood Kids
Summertime on Culverhouse St.

A Church Named Shiloh

Burgundy red brick with steaming
white wooden trim.

Double doors at the entry beckons
you to come within.

Deacons attired in their suits of armor in support
of the pastor in the pulpit stand.

Singing hymns of traditional times and the reverence of
prayers in melodic tones.

Sometimes I don't know what they're saying, but I know it's
Dear Lord invocations for all that hear.

Memories flaunt my mind of speeches my Grandmom mailed
to me, and I shared them in front of the Shiloh church
crowd every year at Easter time.

It was fun singing in the choir directed by Ms. Arnest,
who was always stylish and lead with
an animated theme.

The rows were filled with skilled singers like my
Grandmother and other family; Aunt Cora Lee, Aunt
Catherine, Aunt Bobbye, Uncle Sam and Dede. As well as our
cousins Pat, Emma and Ray.
Shiloh's Pastor, Rev. Dolphus was there for a long time. In fact,
the church street bears his name.
God Bless Shiloh and all its members, as I pray
that it always remains.

Dedicated to
The Greater Shiloh Baptist Church
Lufkin, Texas

The Melon Patch

In the midst of Sweet Union beyond the country roads,
deep in the pines, and a vastness of plush green land lies
a place that's always special to me.

It holds a church and three generations of homes
on the land of our family tree.

The first home seen is Mother Jessie's and Daddy Revous',
great Grandmom's home is next and
then Aunt Minnies.

Surrounding the main house was a stone water well
and three gardens that had different growings.

One hot summer day the children, whom were all
grandchildren, were there to visit.

Outside in the sun, we soaked our bodies full
of vitamin rays and all the fun we could.

We were next to the melon patch.
Melons were growing, dark green stripes
along a lighter green skinned.

My Grandmom came and told us to go to
the patch and pick a melon for each of us!
They were ripe, big and juicy and
ready for the haul.

A few of us thumped for a good one although we didn't
really know what we were doing. If you listen just right,
the sound tells you how ripe and sweet it is.

So we thumped and chose and asked, "what's next?"
"Bust it open, enjoy and eat it!" Grandmom said.

I smile and remember how we thump-thumped away
and busted red melons from the melon patch that day.

*Thank you for that day Mother Jessie and the ancestors that brought us to
Sweet Union, Texas*

The Wrecking Yard

The wrecking yard was an adventurous place,
where my Grandfather worked and most of the livelihood came.

Our garden was rows and rows of mounded dirt, and each row
was filled with a different vegetable.

Piles of rich soils held the bounty of nature that we'd planted
and cared for. Now it was picking time.

Tall, light green corn stalks with yellow corn peeked from
beneath, stretching to the maker of the clouds.

Rows of rich collard greens glistening with growth.

Peas in the pods leaning north to south, all was ready for our
"pull and pick," "pick and pull."

The pigs within their pig pen area run wild, rolling in the
mud, wanting to be wrapped and smothered to make
them feel cool and comforted.

Seeing the little ones with their curly tails were my favorite
thing to do! One day I went closer, before one of the pinkies
"Mama Hog" came barreling towards me and my Aunt Dede.
We had to hop on the car to escape her "snorting and rage!"

"Chrungh-chrungh." "Chrungh!"
"Away from my curly babies!" she squealed.

We escaped somehow with my Grandfather's help. He was so
good about taking care of all things out there.

With buckets of slop, he fed them. The smell of mixed discarded foods brought an odor of sourness, but it was a scrumptious meal for them. And they all rushed, knocking into one another to consume it.

Though the pigpen area was dirty and smelly, I was always ecstatic to visit.

No matter about the stench-like odor or the deathly charging of that Mama Hog, wouldn't deter me.

We weren't allowed inside the pen, but we always climbed up on the fence to get as close as we could!

On the other side of the pigs in the garden on the far left was a cherry plum tree. We gather those golden yellow berries, wipe them off on our shirts, then crunch and taste the sweetness of berry juice.

My Grandfather loved this land that he and my Grandmother owned. He came out amongst these pines and cedar trees towing cars of all kinds to sell the parts from them and kept a pig farm as well as our bountiful garden.

What a life!

Dedicated to
my Grandparents Della Mae & Buster Traylor

Traylor Garden

This area of town was called Cedar Grove, and the wrecking
yard was the area that you drove into.

After the pigpen, we went straight to work in the garden,
which was deeper inside.

Collards, vivid and dark leafy greens, with mustards fanned
out with a lighter olive hue. Golden corn stalks standing
up tall with peas sprouting out next to them.

At picking time, we'd grab plastic bags and pull the peas,
collard greens and corn stalks up.

At home Grandmom shucked the corn from the cob and
we'd help with the snap and peel of the peas.

The greens were cleaned and cooked and then frozen,
along with the fresh corn and peas. It kept until the time
to be pulled out for us to season and serve.

And the family waited patiently for the fair of the good Lord
and what our hands had pulled up from the ground.

The Train that Drowned

Down in East Texas, a tale is often told. Spoken
and whispered far beyond the town and way past
the leaning necks of the giraffes at the Zoo.

Up above the green pines and way past Jones Lake,
where gators roam a street in Lufkin.

There's a sign there that shares a beware of them
crossing the street.

But back to the Tale that happened:

Past this town where I grew up,
was another that was an hour
plus away. Jasper is the place where
there's a wide lake that
many swim in, that's shimmery and blue.

My Mom tells me of a time they went to
this Blue Hole to have
picnics and family time
with my Grandmom, Granddad,
her brother, Aunt Catherine
and my Uncle Talmadge.

And she heard of this tale, about a
long, big train that
slid deep in the blue water.

It broke free from the rails, and
plunged far deep within
this mysterious lake.

It's said that the bottom connects
to a bottomless hole
and whatever slips away, is never seen again.

She said, "It never came out. The train is still there,
in a place where it will never be found."

Tribute to the story of The Blue Hole
Jasper, Texas

Big Mama Made

Big Mama made all things flow for everyone.
Her kindness and generosity never ended.

With eleven children, along with Big Daddy and herself, she
still had a plate to offer a visitor.

Big Mama made flour sack dresses.
The material came from her sacks of flour. When she saw a dress
that she wanted a child or grandchild to have, she'd draw out a
pattern on a paper sack. Then cut it out using it as a pattern.
And then a beautiful dress would be sewn.

Big Mama was so creative; she also cooked and baked a lot.
For holidays, she would bake thirteen different cakes.
One for each child and two extra.

Many flavors deliciously created:
strawberry, chocolate frosting and yellow cake, chocolate
cake with chocolate frosting, fresh coconut with the
boiled white frosting, german chocolate, yummy lemon,
jelly roll, pineapple, fruitcake, butter pound cake
and orange were just a few.

And she also made the best homemade tea cakes in town!

Dedicated to
Big Mama, my Grandmother and the Aunties
who have shared their yummy baking skills with us!

Blues of Life and Love

Freedom Tree

Gotta get up in a tree, so I can be free
Gotta get up in a tree, so I can be free
Gotta get up in a tree, so they can't see me!

Free of the dogs that sniff my trail
Free of the yells making my heart curtail

My feet are torn
They bleed, they ache
Ripped by the ground, as I ran away

My lungs are worn. I strain to make no sound
Body tormented from beatings and pounds

My mind is ablaze. My eyes are all crazed
Mixing with my ancestors', as they
writhe in their graves

Seeking water to cross that river,
I can see my mama cryin'.
She don't want to see another of hers dyin'.

Dogs barkin' louder
No hiding in sight

Gun shots are poppin'
Shanks grab me real tight

Seeing visions of rotting,
my body strung high

Warning for others,
don't run and take flight

They shout,
"Black boy, you wanna run, and flee from me? Then, you
gon' be hung and swung from a tree!"

Snapped to my senses,
my end I can see

Red blood is drainin'
brown neck is hangin'

Strong rope, chokes and cuts
my eyes bulgin' guts

And flooded with tears
'cause mines gonna die
for many more years

Tired, stopped runnin',
they reach me real quick

Ride'n those horses,
helped them do the trick

They circle me round,
kick me to the ground

Tied hands behind back,
beaten, my head cracked

Rope thrown very fast
Jerked to loop and snatch

Strapped tight round my neck,
pulled up with a snap!

Feeling' pain and calm now,
'cause I understand how

My escape is to fly,
as I travel to God's sky

All my life, I was dreamin'
of that sweet, far-off freedom

Which never could be,
'till I swung from a tree.

Dedicated to
the brave man that needed his story to be told

Assassinate Thee

If you cannot be a puppet, we will assassinate thee

You know, just like Martin, Malcolm and Kennedy
You need to follow our rules and step back when we say

Don't go against the grain, or you will be slain
There is a secrecy and psyched up religious order to this
larger platform and the politics of the world

As you trifle with us, we will definitely follow you

Dear Madams and Sirs,

it will be too late to seek help
by then, we've been watching and have a full case study,
painted with *our* colors of you

After then, it won't be long, before
your lights are out and the darkness comes

Innocent Tim Cole

Eighty thousand a year was given to the family at first, now
$160,000 is paid, years after I've gone

My family helped set a law, helping innocents falsely
accused, now to receive this atonement

The Texas Governor gave the decree. No one else like me
will be wrongly accused without being payed this fee

An instituted apology, posted and declared, gurgled from an
injustice placed upon me

Sadness saturated and twisted me inside,
as I prayed and cried day and night for us who were
sentenced, without the proof of a crime

Beg. Suffer. Pray.
My screams were loud, but no justice heard

I served fourteen years, of a twenty-five year
sentence, before dying of a heart attack.

Locked in my cell, though innocent, there was no one to call.
No help for me, no Judge's reprieve

A spook might you be
The diabolical demon of the sentencers' own mind and design.

Newspapers accused me, but failed to seek proof
of my innocence.

Hurled names that made me sick inside
Yet I still prayed for the woman that had been attacked.

I was finally offered parole, if I confessed to the crime,
but I couldn't because I was never guilty.

As an honor, and future law student, I'd always believed
in innocence until proof of guilt
Even shared the motto with my sister who was in law school.

To her I wrote,
"I still believed in Justice, though it
didn't believe in me."

Ode to Tim Cole exonerated after his death

A bronze statue was placed at Texas Tech University
for Timothy Cole where he attended and was
wrongly accused of a crime

White Lies: Part I

The woman who taught me to teach now needs help
to think. She is losing her mind at a sledgehammer
pace, day by day.

For 45 years, she knew what to say in class,
but now she can't recall her name.
She's losing her path.

The woman who taught me to read can't
even remember a word.

The vacuum cleaner has become
the sound: vroom-vroom.
And water is called:
swish-swish.

She has no recollection of
the day of her birth
or the current year when we speak.

And to her, there are no days
of the week.

She's become the student, and I am the teacher
of the woman who taught me to teach.

The days are filled with her continually
asking things over and over.

Today the request is to repeat my name again.
She smiles after hearing, then says,
"Who are you?"

I tell her and she slowly repeats it, never
showing that she's heard it before.

When I answer, she smiles again, and quickly says,
"What do you do? Where do you live?"

I tell her, "I'm Lisa, your granddaughter, an actress and writer in
California. I live in the hills you spoke about
all the time. Remember?"

I'm crossing my fingers, in hopes her brain
will connect the dots.

*"Beautiful hilltops where the legendary Movie
stars live!"* she used to say.

Blank eyes stare back at me, then
"Oh, yes!" she replies.

But I know it is part of her newly
formed white lies.

The ones she's not aware that she tells.
It becomes a quick response that helps her cover
the memory that has failed.

Seasoned Southern Style

Everything in life seems to be a recipe
Never complete measurements written for anything
Its taste is trial and error, season and re-seasoning

A pinch of this, a shake of that
a prayer and blessing tossed on top and an overfill of all our
ancestor's culinary embracement and love

It's when you get that humming in your head and a flavor
bud captured in your mouth and soul. With everything
you bake, fry, sauté, boil or barbecue

When that *Mmm-mm* goodness saturates you all around,
you know you've hit that soaked in
Southern flavorful style

And that my dear,
is the true *Southern way!*

Dedicated to
All Southern Cooks

Must Be Naked

I must be stripped to be seen,
so that the sanctity of pureness, I can reveal
my multi-layers of womanhood and being a Black woman
have packed on and pressed upon within said society

And also what my mother, Grandmothers, ancestral
predecessors have fought for and
expect of me

I must be peeled away, removed like the sturdy yellowed
skin that firmly holds a banana within. Protecting my
insides from being crushed, mashed

When this peeling occurs,
I
will
be
seen,
showcasing the beauty and elegance I behold

Crowing as the loudest rooster around, dancing
the funky chicken, as I flap my flabby arms
with no covering and groove
full out, with robot moves

And then buzzing around carelessly, like a
clumsy black and gold bumble bee

I will prance or pounce any way I like,
ignoring chastisement of the better
way a woman should be in public
and doing things right

My Grandmother can't say, "Uh-uh now, shoosh!
That's too loud." "We don't need to be loud."
Or my Mother, "cross your legs!"

And Elders, "keep your dress down,
and your thighs closed."

I won't have to hold it all together. Piling the layers
up top like balancing pageant walking
books on my head, oh so high

Dress right/don't walk to the right/walk straight/sit poised/
head high/be comfortable/not too relaxed outside/must be
up right/not too uptight/and close the legs/speak fluently,
with niceties/don't say that word/stop saying I caint. It's can't
or can not/no laughing loud/only at home with family should
you thrash about so/don't be loose/or careless or too free/
you can't do that/we can't do that/hold yourself in now

That's why I need the nakedness,
so that I can be the beautiful Black woman I am, human

Being
        just
            me.

Dedicated to
Myself

Soaked in Prowess

I would like to bathe like Esther, preparing myself
with florals, soaked and lavished
for my king.

My body dipped in natural oils to absorb the fragrant
extractions of roses, lavender and ripened
juniper berries.

Presented la 'natural as I am massaged to help complete
a look that's to compel an embracement and
promise from a king.

I want to be like Esther, pampered daily for several months.
Hair glistening and waves bouncing from pomades
by God's nature-prints.

Supple neck and readied bosom, peaking from the caressment
of natural extractions.

With eyes blazingly warm and dark, simmering for the wait of
the special appointment that is to come.

As servants perfect my skin, resulting in glistening shoulders
that becomes soft as buttercream.

Completely and meticulously attended to. From the button
in her belly and beaded jewels around her waist, that
guide you to swirling hips and sculpted thighs.

Down to softened feet and half moon shaped toenails.
After months of this preparation,
Esther's time came.

Her spirit was ablaze with excitement wanting
to be the *chosen one.*

As the king came to seek his one, he saw Esther.
He was enraptured by her beauty.

An energy that magnetized, pulled his spirit to hers.
The mighty power that he had over a kingdom, would soon
be granted unto her.

And while he reigned over Esther, Esther also
reigned over him.

God had orchestrated this, far beyond those prints of nature.

She had been groomed as a gift, and her king had gifted her
with power and a nation. Together they helped to secure
the future of her people.

My favorite story of the power of love and positioning
Book of Esther, Holy Bible

Poetic Flutters

I'm beginning to wonder if I really
know how to write poetry.

Each person's poetic way is so vastly different. Some
of it I comprehend, and others I do not.

What is simplicity?

Too simple, the narrative seems weak indeed. And
one that's more complex seems beyond my reach of
comprehension and or desire to read.

So am I a poet?
This I do not know

I thought I was a long stretch ago, but these days and
moments as I hear the poetic muses speak their
melodies, it seems I have no great symbolic notes
to share. Or no deep stories to unfold.

I shake my head now wondering "What I'm doing here.?"

She is a Jewel

How lovely her stance,
a bust of Roman times from whence she came,
amply named and positioned for her magnificence

Yet like Rome, the suppleness must fall, no
longer awarded for beauty alone, her eternalness
has faded, but exists in its
own gorgeously sumptuous way.

Her beauty and her hue share a familiarity with me,
observing timely radiance amidst the
shimmer of a darkened glow

She is a jewel like me, a beautifully prismed
jewel like me

True Poet

Am I a true Poet?

Of that I don't really know. It comes to me at times, just
as the wind blows, it begins as a breeze.

Yet there are many moments that I'm plucking on the
strings so rough, I feel I'll break a chord or halt the
spiritual flow of things.

Why does it feel like others "feel" so deeply? Or are
haunted by a mystic sending tunes to them?

And I seem to struggle with the beat or sweet
description of a moment in my memory,
I feel distressed.

I have great poets I admire, and I feel
their words and poetic touch is often
not what I am able to pen. I'm too simplistic
at times, and sometimes beyond a
deepness with a history that haunts
me and is not directly mine.

Yet I see some of the greatest poets at times
speak with such simplicity, haunted by feelings
that also weren't their own.
I seem to write of ghosts like
Poe, and is that okay?

This all could be my faith in my gifts or abilities.
The finality? Can I paint a picture that's
filled with lovely fluidity?

And if I can once or twice, with depth of
my spirit's source, then maybe, just maybe,
I can call myself some kind
of poet.

A bona fide, true blue poet.

And I'll finally believe that I'm forever infused
with fluidic and poetic melody.

Beautiful Gift

Dear God,
she has an amazingly beautiful gift,
and no fatal flaws that I see!

Why are there some that God bestows a gift beyond every
measure? And those that strive so earnestly,
but never get close.

Is there a difference made amongst us?

I'm afraid to think about our Father picking favorites.
I accept that all can't glow the brightest upon the path.
While some will lead, others follow.

But I shall glow and show the way,
for I was not made to follow another's sway.

A while ago I was told I had a "gift from Almighty God."

I wonder if that day the one who shared this knew she'd
pushed my spirit further?

I often think of the words imparted to me, and wish I knew
how to be the best that I could be.

But then I suppose the one who bestowed the gift will show me.

Dedicated to
the inspiring and beautiful voice of Kathleen Battle

Let's Stay Together

When asked the question how does one stay in a long-term relationship, my answer is the following:

Eternity of togetherness seems a mystery to most.
It's a gift that's often filled with aches, anguish,
hard to understand and possess. Though it
is possible to be grasped and tucked lovingly away.

Extraction
1. Desiring an embracement of warmth that swirls and infuses every single tip of us, tingling, pulsating and breathless. A stream that continuously moves as it caresses and sometimes topples.

2. A faithful and spiritual belief you share that suits you and grants stability when life and earth ramble simultaneously.

3. Belonging and thriving with a group of spirits that allow you to dance and leap! A rarity we seek when we find those with dreams and thoughts like our own, a tribe.

Spirits melding
4. The connection that helps you breathe, brings forth a pulse of warning and desire. A plateau that reaches true completeness, a euphoria.

5. Souls must blossom side by side, together to have this. Protecting and racing with rigor to garner this existence.

The above is important, for each one's core strength can't be nurtured by only one source pouring within it.

The Secret?
There are sacrifices within this picture.

Said simply
Sometimes your right is not so right at all. Sometimes you
may be wrong, just for someone else's sake.

Like when the roll of toilet paper is requested to be
over or under. Or the bed covers to be pulled up
and over the pillows, then tucked under
or pulled away from the pillows, at least a foot away.

The Sacrifice
Is what brings the bounty of it all so
beautifully together. Cementing the locking
of souls, where those tantalizing glances are
exchanged back-and-forth. And the heat rises,
breathless, pounding from your heart and body.

And eventually you connect the dots and can move
and croon to Al Green's "*Let's Stay Together*"
while seeing the worth of all the sacrifices
in each other's deeply loving eyes.

I Write

I am a writer.
The things I do not say to you, I will write.
If I write,
this means I care. You've hurt me, or I'm
thinking about you.

Either way there's a connection. And powerful juju
if you receive a letter.

When I don't give a damn, you won't receive anything.
Not a glance, a memory.
You are gone. Never existed.

Except for a speck of dust, sliver of hair or eye matta' that I
have cleansed from my inner
eye and discarded.

I Prefer

Emotions
pull us closer, as the pull of hate keeps us stuck. Both can
stagnate, but only one is duly positive.

Ignoring
them simultaneously is said to bring about a combustible
feeling that can only be extinguished by a deep sensual affair
or a deep wound in the back, like a stab.

Myself
I abhor conflict and would rather have passion and love,
picnics and yummy tasting things like tea cakes and berries
or fresh baked scones and clotted cream.

Perfection
is a balanced day of good temperature and wind flow. And the
scents of fresh rain and honeysuckle surrounding me.

Episodes
like this can be alone, as I am content to spend time with my
deeper self. Or with a beautiful-spirited soul, either my mate
or a long lost lovely friend.

Dedicated to
my lovely Knight with the dark brown eyes

My Artistry

I met a poet today.

She recognized me from something else,
and it was not my poetry.

I had to explain I was a poet too. I'd always been a poet, but I
had paused my "poetetness" for some reason.

"Maybe happiness?" she said, and I understood, for I always
wrote melancholy poetry in the past.

Yet I thought her statement was funny, and a bit ironic for me
because it was actually during the worst times in my life when
I'd almost succumbed to death, that I had stopped writing.

And that's a puzzle to me still. Why would I be silent during
the most difficult, gut wrenching, needing-to-bare-my-soul
times in my lifespan?

I'm clearly a mixed up artistry-type of soul that has no rhyme
or reason really.

But to simply share when I want to,
and simply refuse when I don't.

Visions of my Languages

In learning different languages, whether linguistically or within your soul, everything echoes with all that is wrapped within you.

English is my 1ˢᵗ language.

Spanish zips through me at times in my second brain. And then I see forms and movements as my third language, in American Sign Language.

Love is like that to me, wrapping me with many facets like a lavishly beautiful cloak or a warm cuddly blanket.

My Love is shared in these two languages and interpreted in the third language when performed live and in person.

Here is Mi' Amor

Mi' Amor

The poetry of his love holds me close,
as it zooms within my heart like tiny arrows.
It is him I'll always adore and call "mi amor."

Mi' Amor II

La poesía de su amor me mantiene cerca,
a medida que se acerca a mi corazón,
como pequeñas flechas.
Es a 'él a quien siempre adorare' y llamaré' "mi amor."

Love Score

I did not know what love was to be,
but it was in the ways that you cared for me and you showed
me that I learned what it ought to be.

I didn't have this in my life before. I had to fend for
myself and figure things out. I had always been the fixer of all
that had strife, so when you came into my life it
was different. Where was your strife?

You were wired to give, and it took me a while to
embrace this on the receiving end, but when I realized
all you'd been doing for me, I understood reciprocity
and the desire to take care of others needs,
along with your own, no matter what.

That is a part of what loving and living meant, and now we
have this love thing "down."

Together, we're hot boulders on fire, high scorers and spikers.

With love to you for always and forever,

xo
Vixen

Dedicated to
My brown eyed Knight

Digging a Well

Stop making well check calls,
placing loved ones of color to be "well" put in a tomb.

The name "well" plainly states, and
foretells the steps that will be taken

Well done, sir! Is that how you'd like them
prepared today, sir?

We know of the disappearances of bodies
found long ago and today.

Thrown to their end, in a darker darkness, deep
down in the dirt of earth.

Surrounded by mortar after being
led down to a well.

So now you give them permission by
requesting a Well check?

Their reply, *we'll have*
this well done for you.

Next, you go pick your burial site,
like the times when we took care and

threw them in a well and
covered them up, deep down below.

We can darken their darkest days for you
and it will be Well done!

STOP!

calling for a well check
unless you know they are already dead!

We need no more seasoning of the rotten waters,
no more Brown and Black bodies tossed and filled in.

#vanessamarquez
#atatianakjefferson

Strength of the Butterfly

That little butterfly is holding on,
oblivious to all the turbulence.

Holding on for dear life amidst all the strife.

As its wings close and flutter, my heart begins to slowly
unclutter, for I realize that I, much larger than
that butterfly, can hold on just the same to
fight my battles.

Hold on for dear life, amidst all the strife.

I look up and see the butterfly has released it's hold
and its presence on the flower is no longer there.

It is a sign from God.

Time for me to remove my presence, venturing on,
encompassed with the wind, and to survive.

With new breath, there is life!

A Dignified Death, Please

I would like a dignified death, please.
I refuse to leave here, in absence of it.

My mother often said, "if you get into an accident or
something happens, you must always
have on clean underwear."

So change my undies if they're dirty or have any unseemly
holes or rips and make sure they fit just right,
no overfills or too uptight, if you know what I mean.

I've oft been taught, for my mother's sake
and mine, this is the ultimate rule.

The home must be pristine before any entrances from
outsiders are made. If this is not the case, you
are not to answer the door.

If you do, you must step outside and speak
to them there.

Now this was no joking matter when I was
young. Or even now, as I am older.

It could be a million dollar check being delivered
to our door, and that check would not have
been seen unless the house is squeaky clean!

"Spotless before anyone enters" has been
the rule since I can remember.

So receive this upon a bodily revelation
of me and this request.

No ambulance or resuscitators allowed until
the cleaning of all quarters and corners of
the house is completed and done.
This is the 1st and beginning
of my list.

Oh, you may laugh, but it's truly embedded
within my spirit and in my head.

My husband promised this to me a long, long time ago.
I don't know if he'll stick to it. I do hope
that he will abide.

It's not so hard you see, I *plainly and must*
be allowed and given this courtesy. I would
like a dignified death, please.

I must not have my hair sticking up all over
the place. It must be combed, brushed,
coiffed in some way or neatly pulled
down or laid back somehow.

My face cannot look like it's been stuck in shock
mode like a mackachoo or crazy road lizard.
You know those that have been darting
'to and fro' from traffic in the
road with eyes ablaze?

And the shakes of a bewildered person going through a
tough withdrawal of something that they've
been feigning for or lost.

And as my Grandfather would say, "wash
the 'matta out my eyes' and make my
face fresh and clean."

No need for makeup. It's fine to do a
soap and water cleanse. Fresh, clean
and lightly moisturized.

We don't want dry-ashy, skin-flaking or
drooping wrinkly-jowls of any kind.

Just let me have dignity in death, please.

I suppose they will not part my lips, unless
they are giving me 'mouth to mouth,' so maybe
I'd like to have my teeth cleaned? And a
bit freshened as well.

Not that strong smelling alcohol Listerine scent that I recall
growing up with or that sickening smell of
bubblegum sweetness.

Just clean teeth and unfunked breath,
if that can be done. If not, I'm good,
as long as 'you can be.'

And Dear God, don't let my legs be hairy with
long thick wisps of black hair showing down
my carmel thick legs. Not my toenails left
unkempt and jutting out like
an owl's claws.

The nails don't have to be polished. As you know, in reality,
they rarely ever are, so I don't expect
something in death that I don't in life.

But I don't want to cut someone, like I sometimes have cut
my dear husband's leg in bed, as he's complained about a long
unkempt self-care spell.

And what if I ripped the bag the orderlies zip me up in? Just
a quick 'straight across' toenail clip will suffice. I'm really not
that picky, as long as you can do me right.

Just let me be dignified in my death.

I refuse to die in the absence of it.
Oh! If you'd like – not that I request –

you could add a little face powder that matches the
tone of my skin and a tint of something
lightly on my lips.

But, I guess those things aren't that important and can
be done in prep time for the final stage.

So forget that part, just clean my face in
the way that I stated first.

And finally, make sure that there's no hair
Anywhere that shouldn't be.

I don't want to be spread out and ogled upon,
with strands of hair growth that have sprouted
beyond the closure of my thighs,
way beyond the bikini line.

Or flying below the safe zone of my armpits. Or
wild hairs on my chin, chest or too wild a union of the
brow, like my lady Ms. Frida Khalo.

I would be stared at for too long, because I get lots
of puffy-hair beyond my times of non-shaving
winter months, and I don't Brazilian wax!

I don't want
anyone in that area except me, my
husband and sometimes my Gyno for a
check-up and pap smear.

Remember to pass upon that traditional dead body in
the casket burial. Because I don't like that.

Comply with my cremation request and a dedicated picture
on an easel or a table top, with a toasting
of rose' or juice and strawberries served
with strawberry cake!

After people speak of the good times they've shared with
me and the strength and beauty I had as a person, move along
in the procession of the day.

Spread my cremated ashes where you feel, so I can
rest and be in peace for the long haul.

This is the step by step of a
Dignified death, of my request.

Dedicated to
anyone who finds me in my demise

Red Lips

I wonder what I'll look like when I'm dead.
Will my face be painted red?
Will they look at me and say, she was
a beauty in her day?

Then shout for joy for my travel to the saints
or cry with fervour for the loss of
my spirit?

Will they follow all my orders and set things
up as I desired?

What will I look like when I'm dead?
Will I be thin or swole?
In the casket will I smell?

Will I wear a wig or will they do my hair just right?
And will I sleep deeply or hear their wails and
comments as I float into the sky?

Does it matter what I look like to them or me?
Death is final, no do overs for that time, it's just the end,
where we say goodbye.

Grateful

Strong One

Such a sight I'll remember, less than 2 years old.
Walking down the hospital corridor,
your hand holding the IV pole.

Bringing smiles and happiness like a boomerang,
your spirit was filled with positive light.

You smiled at every nurse that we passed by.
I was worried for you to be there that young,
but you showed such strength within yourself.

Another time, you were almost gone,
such a fighter within you and a drive for life.
You've always kept a pace to win.

A loyal spirit and steadfast friend,
my favorite listener till the end,
my little brother shines so bright,

I will always admire your stamina and fight.
God blessed with a friend and a little brother to love,
we shall dance together through this journey of life,
winning and shining our family light!

J baby,
you are cherished and loved forever.

Picture Exhibit 1

**My growing up years.
Ponytails "Pigtails" forever!**

Felicia growing up years

Picture Exhibit 2

**Strong Family
Grandparents, Parents &
Grandmom's**

Buster & Della Mae Traylor, James & Ruth Taylor
and Revous & Jessie Bell Taylor

Picture Exhibit 3

Both Grandmom's, Parents, Family & me

James & Ruth Taylor, Felicia Taylor, Pat & Chris Peacock, Deirdre & Della Mae Traylor, Charlotte Traylor & Kay Kimble, Revous "Sonny" Taylor & Jessie B. Taylor, Laurance Traylor & Ruth Taylor

Picture Exhibit 4

Blessed with my brothers after 10 years of being an only child

Felicia, Jason & James Taylor Jr.

Creative One

Burst of energy and deep down love,
expressions are full of beaming light
with a bounty of skills he does possess.

Crafting, cooking, drawing and mathematical skills.
Reading, writing stories and drawing creatively, athletic
and strong with amazing handstands and timed runs.

He's such a Renaissance man!
My favorites are his laughter and his artistic pizzazz.
And his big, bold and bright,
love-burst, pounding heart.

He pushes hard to get things done.
There's moments it's blurry and takes him extra time,
but it's always beautiful at the finish line.

His spirit consumed my love at first sight!
Dear precious Lord, thank you for his life.
I see him blossoming grander than his vision can be.

Big hugs to him, for I'll always have him
wrapped in my heart that's filled with love.

Love you *most & more,*
my big and little *Nicholas*

Appreciation

Nse for your forever love, support and encouragement. And pushing me to journey in this Book publishing path against all odds.

Nicholas for joyful inspiration, kindness and love hugs. And being my soundboard and word provider.

Mom & Dad for teaching me and my brothers that we're capable of anything we work for and God will work out the rest! And your forever love and support.

Brother Jason for always listening, loving and saying "You can do it, Sis!"

Grandmom Della Mae for encouraging me to write books. And she and my Grandfather always gave me a happy place with love and support.

Dede for playing with me and sharing her friends with me, when I was younger.

Cass and Bebe for your forever sister support and love.

Friends for their positivity, love and steadfast spirits.

Angels Jamie, "Daddy" Buster, Mother Jessie & Daddy Revous.

Aunties for always having a positive spirit to share and delicious desserts in your kitchens for everyone.

Uncles for giving advice and showing the family such positive role models.

Ancestors Big Mama's, Big Daddys, Uncles, Aunties

Professor Hiram for guidance and sharing your passion for the poet's path. And the vision of stepping into it and helping me dream further.

CLI Staff and Students for your support, inspiring poetry and wonderful assistance. And Mr. DeWayne whose poetry pushed me to be more.

World Stage Press Thank you for your "belief in me" and your continued support! And **Jerry** for your patience in my many questions. For **Krystle's** designing eye and dedication, **John's** detail and great comments. And appreciation to **Jade** and **Michelle's** designs along this path.

Aimee Bender for unknowingly inspiring my poetry path and never forgetting my Crawdad story.

Los Angeles Poet Society, DSTLA, Rio de mi Vida Writers, Poets & Writers, Telling Your Truth Workshop I would have perished without the outlet of creative writing workshops you share with the community and make possible for us to participate in. Along with each of your gifts of ongoing positivity. You're all blessings!

Nieces, Nephews, Goddaughter and Godsisters may you find stories to share forever and find inspiration within my writing.

Cousins Traylor, Taylor, Johnson, Penson and Odoms. Thank you for the continued love, the family times, online and texting talks.

I can not forget **Dr. Winston**, my college poetry Professor at Texas Woman's University that gave me a newspaper clipping of **Maya Angelou's** Inauguration Poem to inspire me.

All of **Maya Angelou's** works speak to and inspire me, including her cookbook where I can even hear her voice as I read and cook.

Thank you for the **Reviews** and for sharing your thoughts about my work:

Michael Fritzen Gratitude for your amazing words and support.

John Crabtree Grateful for your support and sharing your beautiful thoughts.

Karo Ska Gratitude for you in the poetry realm and your support and lovely share.

And the original book of **Langston Hughes** that helped inspire my poetry journey in Los Angeles and taught me the Blues and song of poetry.

"Ain't got nobody in all this world, ain't got nobody but myself. I'm gonna quit my cryin' and put my troubles on the shelf."

The Weary Blues
By Langston Hughes

Avour

Thank you for going on this journey with me!

This was the 1st drawing and vision for the cover of
Southern Spiced: A Brown Girl's Tale

Author Bio

Felicia Taylor E. is a creative that expresses through writing and performance. She enjoys writing poetry and has been leading poetry and performance workshops for over a decade. Her poetry and prose has been published in the *Los Angeles Poetry Anthology*, *Concha's y Cafe Zines*, and the *Heroes de Los Angeles Anthology*. Her poetry and story performances have been presented at *The Huntington Library and Arts Museum, the USC Pacific Asia Museum and Pasadena Museum of History*.

She believes in the healing art of writing, and has helped create plays and facilitated writing workshops with *Imagination Workshop*, an organization by created by playwright Lyle Kessler and actress Margaret Ladd for patients in the UCLA Psychiatric Department and at-risk students. Felicia was raised in Texas and now lives in Los Angeles with her husband and son. She has a passion for baking, collecting old recipes and discovering tea rooms with her family. She studied Journalism and has a BA from Texas Woman's University.

Southern Spiced: A Brown Girl's Tale is her first book of poetry.

www.southernspicedabrowngirlstale.com
IG: @feliciae_writer / IG: @feliciataylore
Twitter: @feliciataylore_